YOUTH BASEBALL HITTING FUNDAMENTALS
A COACH'S GUIDE

ED GARRETSON
COACH AND INSTRUCTOR

American Literary Press, Inc.
Five Star Special Edition
Baltimore, Maryland

Youth Baseball Hitting Fundamentals — A Coach's Guide

Copyright © 2003 Ed Garretson

All rights reserved under International and
Pan-American copyright conventions.
No part of this book may be reproduced, stored in a retrieval system, or transmitted in any form, electronic, mechanical, or other means, now known or hereafter invented, without written permission of the publisher. Address all inquiries to the publisher.

Library of Congress
Cataloging in Publication Data
ISBN 1-56167-796-5

Library of Congress Card Catalog Number:
2002117437

Published by

American Literary Press, Inc.
Five Star Special Edition
8019 Belair Road, Suite 10
Baltimore, Maryland 21236

Manufactured in the United States of America

ACKNOWLEDGMENTS

The author wishes to acknowledge the efforts and assistance of the following individuals in the preparation of this handbook:

    Michael O'K Garretson — demonstrator

    Michael J. Garretson — hitting coach and photographic consultant

    Dan Garretson — CD preparer

    Roger Friedman — editing services

ED GARRETSON
YOUTH BASEBALL EXPERIENCE

COACHED LITTLE LEAGUE MAJORS -
    ASMARA, ETHIOPIA — 1964, 1965

PRESIDENT LITTLE LEAGUE - ASMARA, ETHIOPIA — 1965

COACHED LITTLE LEAGUE MAJORS -
    SPRINGFIELD, VA — 1967, 1968, 1969

COACHED BABE RUTH LEAGUE -
    FORT MONMOUTH, N.J. — 1971, 1972

COACHED BABE RUTH MAJOR LEAGUE -
    SPRINGFIELD, VA — 1973, 1974

COACHED SINGLE A LITTLE LEAGUE -
    SPRINGFIELD, VA — 1980

COACHED DOUBLE A LITTLE LEAGUE -
    SPRINGFIELD, VA — 1981

COACHED TRIPLE A LITTLE LEAGUE -
    SPRINGFIELD, VA — 1982

COACHED LITTLE LEAGUE MAJORS -
    SPRINGFIELD, VA — 1983, 1984

HITTING INSTRUCTOR BABE RUTH 13 YEAR OLDS -
    SPRINGFIELD, VA — 1985

HITTING INSTRUCTOR BABE RUTH MAJOR LEAGUE -
    SPRINGFIELD, VA — 1986

COACHED DOUBLE A LITTLE LEAGUE -
    SPRINGFIELD, VA — 1987, 1988

COACHED T-BALL -
    SPRINGFIELD, VA — 1993, 1994

COACHED DOUBLE A LITTLE LEAGUE -
SPRINGFIELD, VA   1995, 1996

COACHED HITTING -
SPRINGFIELD, VA ALL STARS   1996

CONDUCTED LITTLE LEAGUE COACHES HITTING CLINICS

HERNDON LITTLE LEAGUE   1984

WEST SPRINGFIELD LITTLE LEAGUE   1986, 1990, 1993,
                                                                                  1994, 1995, 1996,
                                                                                  1997, 1998, 1999,
                                                                                  2000, 2001

YOUTH BASEBALL
HITTING FUNDAMENTALS

FOREWORD:

With over twenty years of official involvement in youth baseball, I have come to the conclusion that coaching hitting is one of the most challenging elements of the game. Most coaches are knowledgeable enough to teach fielding, pitching, catching, base running and the rules of the game, but few seem to be skilled in teaching hitting. I believe that hitting is close to 50% of the game. This handbook is more comprehensive than existing sports literature on the fundamentals of hitting. It also presents recommendations and facts on how to coach young hitters.

This handbook is directed toward those managers and coaches who would like some ideas and recommendations that will help them teach and train their teams. It is written to help 5 to 12 year olds by suggesting ways to present them with the fundamentals at a level they can understand and build on as they gain experience.

What knowledge and success I have accumulated over the years is from other coaches, my own coaching experience and input from my four sons who love the game as much as I do.

The author recognizes the participation of female players and coaches in youth baseball programs. Wherever the use of "he", "him", "his", "himself" appear in this handbook, it should be understood that female pronouns could be substituted. This makes the reading of this text simpler without effecting the meaning.

INTRODUCTION:

Hitting a baseball is not the most difficult skill in sports. In fact, hitting a pitched ball during a time at bat is not only possible, but highly probable, given adequate training and practice. This handbook is a collection of facts, rules, suggestions and opinions on the subject of hitting. It is offered as a teaching and learning vehicle for youth league managers, coaches and participating parents. It is written at the fundamental level with the practicalities and realities of coaching youngsters between the ages of 5 and 12. It is based on the premise that understanding the factors that are fundamental to hitting is half of becoming a successful hitter. The other half is, of course, the execution.

For example, young hitters are not sure of what is expected of them in terms of clear and achievable goals. Is it not striking out? Is it batting over .300? Is it getting on base over half the time? How can he measure success (or failure)? As a coach, what should you tell your players you want them to accomplish at bat? I always tell my hitters that they should hit any ball that is going to be called a strike and refrain from swinging otherwise. Whatever the objectives are that you set for your hitters, they inherently become your objectives too. You can measure your own success as a coach by how quickly your players learn, and how well they execute the fundamentals.

The following chapters present material that should help you develop a successful program for your team.

Contents

AUTHOR'S COACHING EXPERIENCE v
FOREWORD vii
INTRODUCTION ix

CHAPTER 1
RULES AND REGULATIONS 1

CHAPTER 2
HITTING FUNDAMENTALS 3

CHAPTER 3
TEACHING FUNDAMENTALS 25

CHAPTER 4
HITTING PSYCHOLOGY 27

CHAPTER 5
PHYSICAL CONDITIONING 29

CHAPTER 6
HITTERS TYPICAL PROBLEMS
AND RECOMMENDED SOLUTIONS 30

CHAPTER 7
PRACTICE - PRACTICE - PRACTICE ! ! ! 33

CHAPTER 9
SUMMARY 43

CHAPTER 1

RULES AND REGULATIONS:

The following rules are extracted and simplified from the official regulations and playing rules of youth baseball.

THE BATTER:
- Must bat in line-up order.
- Must enter batter's box promptly.
- Shall not leave the box after the pitcher sets or winds up.
- Must have both feet in batter's box (lines are in).

THE BATTER IS OUT WHEN:
- A fly ball is caught.
- A third strike is caught or not caught.
- The ball is bunted foul on third strike.
- An infield fly is declared.
- The batter attempts to hit at third strike and is touched by the ball.
- A fair ball touches the batter before the fielder.
- A ball is hit twice in fair territory.
- A runner intentionally deflects the ball.
- Upon hitting a fair ball, the runner does not reach first base before the ball is caught by the first baseman while he touches the base.
- He runs to first base inside of the base line or outside of the three foot line during the last half of the base

path.
- A preceding runner intentionally interfered with the defensive player.
- He steps from one box to the other when pitcher is set.
- He interferes with catcher's fielding or throwing.
- He bats out of turn.
- He hits while one or both feet are out of the batter's box.

CHAPTER 2

HITTING FUNDAMENTALS:

Hitter's Objective:

Ultimately the hitter is successful when he makes contact with the ball and hits it out of the reach of the defense and gets on base. The ideal hit is a line drive through or over the infield and away from the outfielders.

Selecting the Right Bat:

The selection principle is that the bat should be controllable by the hitter according to his size and strength. At the beginning of the practice season and when official league games start, a light bat should be used. Batting gloves are recommended. The size of the batter's hand and the length of his fingers determine the handle thickness of the bat. As the hitter gains bat control and strength, a slightly larger bat can be used. The following table is a recommended size spread according to the hitter's age.

Age	Recommended Bat Size (inches)
5 - 6	24 - 27
7 - 8	26 - 29
9 - 10	28 - 31
11 - 12	29 - 32

As far as the weight of the bat is concerned, the lighter the bat, the more control and the faster the bat-head speed at contact. The heavier the bat, the more difficult it is to control.

SAFETY:

Batters and runners are required to wear batting helmets during practices and games. Helmets prevent injuries as well as protect the managers and league from liability issues.

POSITION IN THE BATTER'S BOX:

The batter's box for youth baseball ages 5 to 12 is 3' by 6' and is centered on the middle of home plate (Figure 2). The batter should position himself in the center of the box (front to rear). He then should position himself at a distance from the plate (Figures 3 and 4) so that he can hit a pitch thrown-on either the outside or inside of the strike zone. More accurately, he must be able to hit any ball that is going to be in the hit zone (Figure 8). Later on in the season, the coach may want to modify a batter's position for such things as a pitcher's throwing speed, game situation or weakness in the defense.

THE GRIP:

Once in the batter's box, the hitter should position his hands on the handle of the bat (Figure 5). The bat should be held across the base of the fingers - not in the crook of the thumb. The hands should be together above the knob of the bat for best control. The grip should be relaxed until the swing is initiated and tightest at the moment of contact with the ball.

STANCE:

Once the batter has addressed the plate as discussed above, he should align his feet parallel to home plate and the long axis of the batter's box (Figure 6). His feet should be spread approximately the width of his shoulders. His knees should be slightly bent and the majority of his weight should be on his rear foot. He should balance himself on the balls of his feet. He elevates the bat until his hands are shoulder high. His wrists are cocked in readiness for his swing. The bat is held so that his arms will become fully extended upon contact with the ball. He then turns his head toward the pitcher by sighting over his forward shoulder.

STRIKE ZONE:

The definition of the strike zone (Figure 7) is that space over home plate that is between the batter's armpits and the top of the knees when the batter assumes a natural stance. The umpire, however, will determine the strike zone according to the batter's size and usual stance when he swings at a pitch.

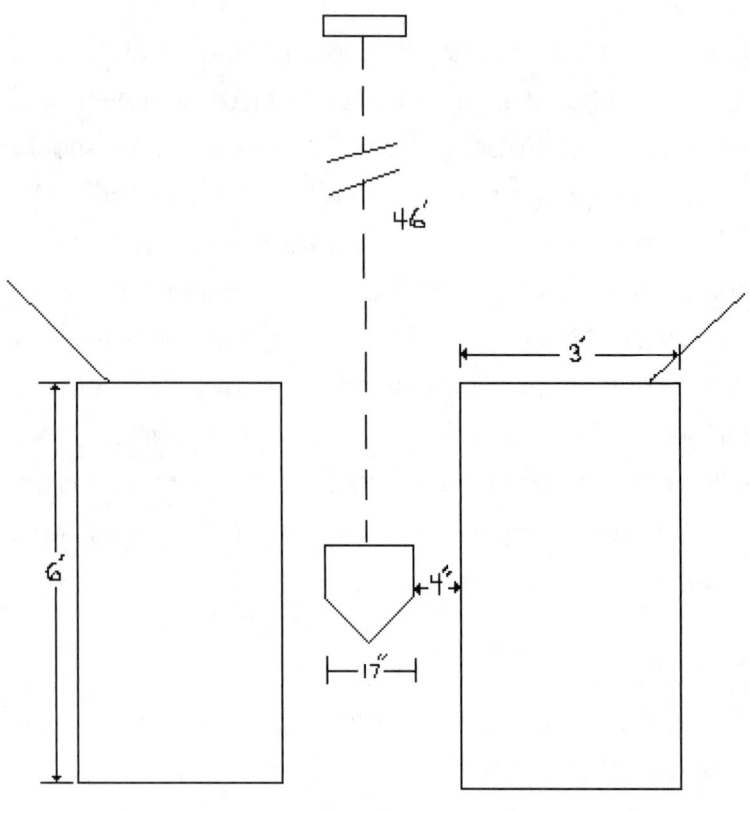

FIGURE 2

Batter's Box Dimensions

FIGURE 3

Position in Batter's Box (front view)

FIGURE 4

Position in Batter's Box (side view)

FIGURE 5

Batter's Grip

FIGURE 6

Batter's Stance

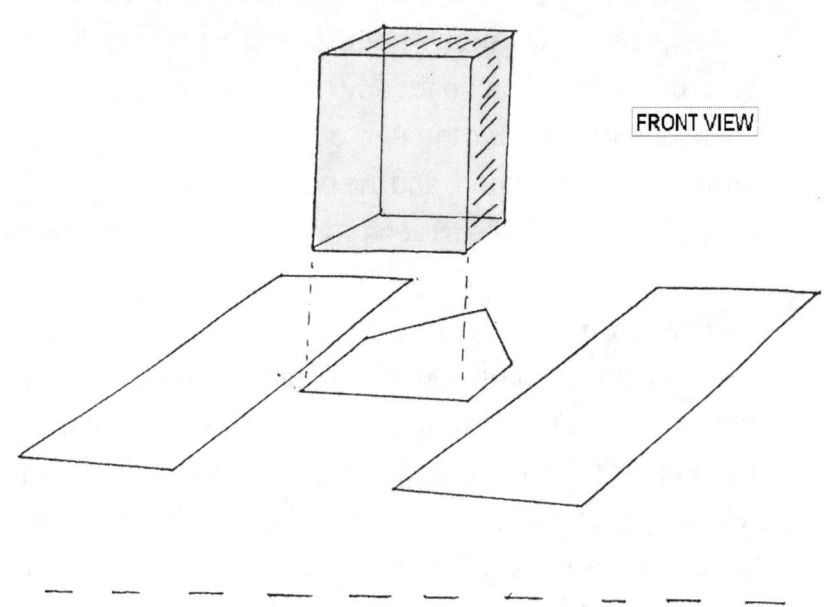

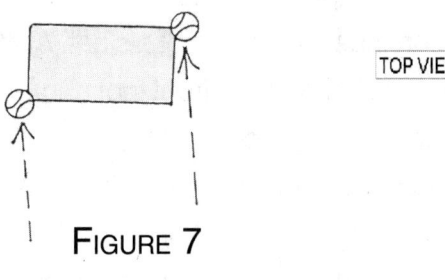

FIGURE 7

Strike Zone

Hit Zone:

The hit zone (Figure 8) is distinguished from the strike zone in that it is the area where contact is made with the ball. Ideally the hit zone for any hitter is that area where contact is made near the end of the swing, the hitter's arms are fully extended, and the bat head has reached its maximum velocity. The hit zone is in front of the strike zone.

The Swing:

Once the hitter has positioned himself in the batter's box and has assumed his stance as described above, he prepares for his swing. He should start his swing (Figure 9) as if every pitch could be a strike. He then checks his swing only if the pitch is not going to be a strike. If the oncoming pitch is going to be a strike, he strides towards the path of the ball with his front foot (Figure 10) and continues the swing of his bat. At this point, his weight begins to shift onto his front foot (Figure 11). His shoulders and hips should then start to uncoil (Figure 12) and drive the bat toward the hit zone. With the bat having been held shoulder high, the track is a shallow downward arc that levels off in the hit zone. The hitter straightens his elbows, reaches forward for the ball and uncocks his wrists. He then pivots his rear foot and completes his swing by following through as his body finishes its turn. The head should remain still throughout the swing to help the batter judge the exact flight of the ball from its point of release all the way to where contact is made.

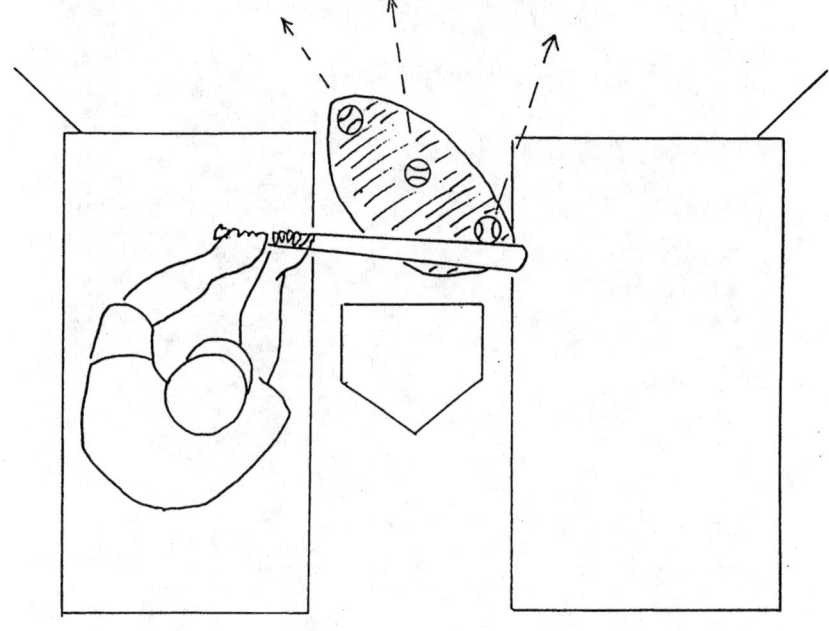

FIGURE 8

The Hit Zone

FIGURE 9

Start of Swing

FIGURE 10

Stride Toward the Path of the Ball

FIGURE 11

Shift Weight Forward

FIGURE 12

Uncoil Shoulders and Hips

PITCHER'S RELEASE POINT:

A pitched ball reaches the batter in just seconds from the time it is released. It is essential that the hitter locate the ball as it is being released from the pitcher's hand (Figure 13) so that the hitter can track the ball through its entire flight. A pitcher's release point can be determined by closely observing his motion during his warm-up or while he is pitching to other hitters The hitter must focus on the expected point of release and not on the pitcher (Figure 14). The hitter should concentrate on seeing the ball coming out of the pitcher's hand. This "release point/ tracking" principle is the most important of all hitting fundamentals. None of the previously mentioned fundamentals will have much value if the hitter doesn't find the ball at its point of release and track it during its entire flight. If a hitter waits to find the ball after it is on its way, his chances of hitting the ball squarely are very slim.

FIGURE 13

Hitter Locates Pitcher's Release Point

FIGURE 14

Pitcher's Release Point

BUNTING:

There are two kinds of bunts authorized in youth baseball. Bunts are not allowed at the 5-T, T-Ball or at any level where the batting Tee is used. The two kinds of bunts are the bunt for a base hit and the sacrifice bunt. They are fundamentally set up and executed the same way. There are several different variations on how to bunt. This method is considered to be the easiest to execute and the safest.

- The bunter positions himself in the batter's box and assumes the hitter's stance as described earlier.
- At the beginning of the pitcher's wind-up, the bunter rotates his feet 90° so that he's facing the pitcher from the front of the batter's box (Figure I5). Bunting from the front of the box will help keep the ball in fair territory.
- He slides his top hand up the bat to a point no further than midway, keeping his thumb and fingers behind the bat so they won't be hit. The bottom hand continues to grip the bat handle firmly.
- The bunter then tracks the ball from the pitcher's release point and prepares to bunt. If the ball is not going to be a strike, he must then pull the bat back to prevent being charged with a strike.
- The bunter then holds the bat firmly with arms extended forward. He guides the bat to the ball and lets the ball hit the bat while holding it parallel to the ground.

FIGURE 15

Bunter's Ready Position

- The bunter's objective is to bunt the ball down the first base or third base lines, mid-way between the catcher, third baseman, first baseman and pitcher. (Figure 16). A bunt towards third base is preferred because the fielder's throw to first base is longer.
- The only difference between a sacrifice bunt and a bunt for a base hit is that the bunt for a base hit is executed after the pitch is on its way. The bunter attempts to deceive the fielders and gain an advantage in reaching first base before the defense can react.

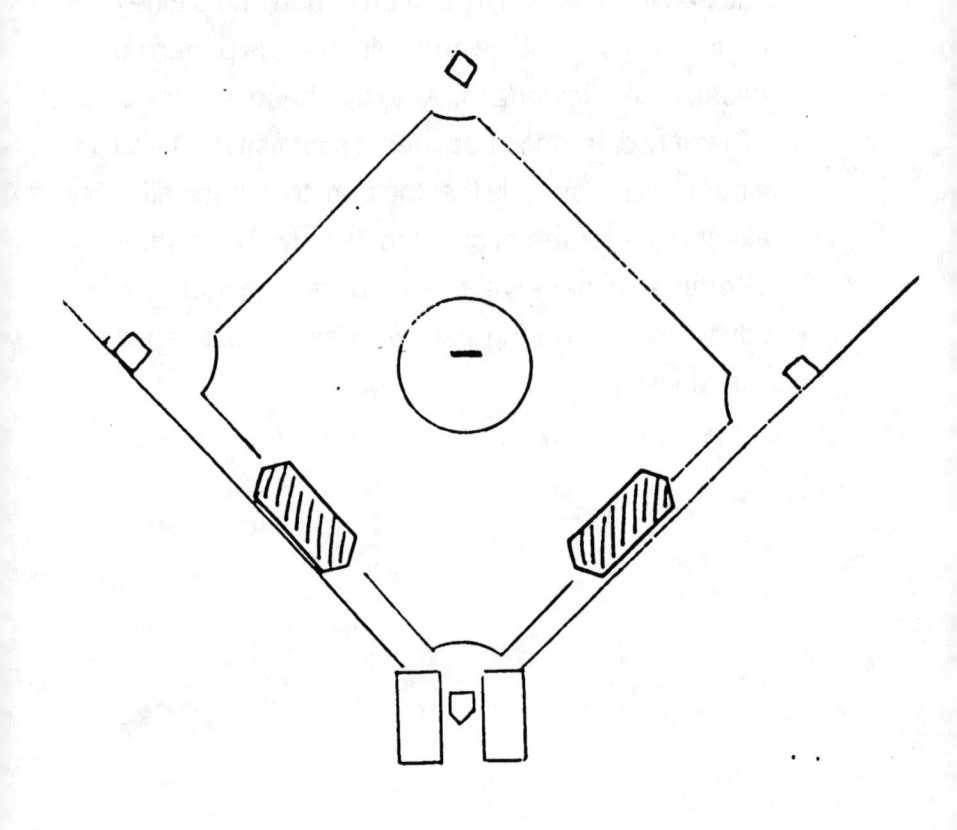

FIGURE 16

Bunter's Targets

CHAPTER 3

TEACHING FUNDAMENTALS

Assuming that a coach understands the hitting fundamentals, how does he go about teaching his players? There are many factors to consider before developing a teaching plan for the season. Here are some questions to address:

- How much time is available for training before and during the season?
- What practice fields / areas are available?
- How old/mature are the players?
- How much experience / knowledge do they already have?
- How much detail can these players understand, absorb, retain and apply?
- Which players need special / extra attention?
- How much help can the coach get from the league (clinics)?
- How much help can be expected from parents or volunteers?

The younger the players the less you expect them to learn and apply. The coaching challenge then becomes finding the most practical mix of level of detail time, players' ability and coaching help. Also obvious is that the amount of time devoted to the teaching of hitting/ offense must be shared with the time allotted to instructing defensive skills and pitching.

CHAPTER 4

HITTING PSYCHOLOGY:

There are some players who have a significant problem making contact with the ball when first exposed to live pitching. They may be able to hit Dad's toss of the tennis ball or practice ball in the back yard but they cannot make contact with a hardball at practice or during a game. They seem to do everything right - their stance seems okay, they appear to be concentrating properly, and their swing is enthusiastic - but all they hit is air. Not only does this happen at the beginning of the season but also it can occur for no apparent reason in the middle of the season. The latter case is usually called a slump, but the conditions are almost identical. These kids did not suddenly lose their hand-to-eye coordination. It most likely is a mental/psychological situation such as trouble at home, peer pressure, parental pressure, fear of being hit by the ball, fear of stinging the hands, etc. These players have to be taken aside and given special attention by the batting coach and/or his helpers. Fear of being hit by a pitch is probably the most difficult problem to overcome. Locating the pitcher's release point and tracking the ball during its entire flight will help alleviate this fear.

Restoration of self-confidence is related to overcoming fear. The first thing to determine is whether the player has listened, absorbed, and is attempting to apply the fundamentals. Review the fundamentals and have him demonstrate every one several times to reinforce his understanding. Use a batting Tee and have him hit balls into a backstop or screen. Then toss him some plastic practice golf balls until he makes contact regularly. These two drills can be conducted by either coaches or volunteers. They can (and should) also be done at home in between practices. Again, the objective is to restore self-confidence through your support and encouragement at practices and at home.

CHAPTER 5

PHYSICAL CONDITIONING

The purpose of physical conditioning is to prevent serious injury to ball players during practices and games. Exercises that are particularly appropriate for hitters are:
- Jogging, running and sprinting
- Stretching and calisthenics
- Upper body strengthening

Jogging at the beginning of practices and games is to loosen leg muscles and stimulate circulation. Running and sprinting should develop progressively, with care not to cause pulled hamstrings or other running muscles.

Stretching and calisthenics should precede practices and games with the objective of preparing muscles for full-speed activities. Stretching leg muscles, trunk muscles, shoulders, elbows and wrists prevent injuries.

Upper body strengthening exercises are essential for the development of hitting power and bat control. The best exercises for the upper body are push-ups and pull-ups. Push-ups can be done on or off the practice field. Pull-ups can be done on school playgrounds and where bars are near by.

CHAPTER 6

HITTER'S TYPICAL PROBLEMS AND RECOMMENDED SOLUTIONS

The following are problems that are common at all levels of the game. Problems, causes and recommended solutions are offered for your consideration.

- Bailing out is striding away from the pitch for fear of getting hit by the ball. The batter will have trouble hitting a ball on the outside of the plate. He must overcome fear through one-on-one drills to improve self-confidence. The batter should be instructed how to properly avoid getting hit by a wild pitch.

- Turning the head is usually caused by the hitter trying to swing too hard, thus losing sight of the pitch just before it reaches the hit zone. Recommend closing the hitter's stance, shortening his stride, and keeping his head still. The batter should concentrate and attempt to see the bat hit the ball.

- Overstriding frequently results in fly balls and pop-ups. A long stride lowers the hitter's body just before contact with the ball. Recommend widening his stance and/or shortening the length of his swing.

- <u>Lunging</u> at the ball is usually the result of the hitter not seeing the ball until well after it has been pitched. The batter tries to make up the lost time by diving at the ball at the last moment. Recommend drills to emphasize seeing the ball leave the pitcher's hand and tracking it to the hit zone.

- <u>Instability</u> is the improper movement of the hitter during set-up and swing preparation. The hitter shuffles his feet and loses stability and concentration. The hitter must anchor his back foot by putting most of his weight over that foot at set-up and the beginning of his swing. He should then push off his back foot and transfer his weight to the front foot as he strides to the ball.

- <u>Hitching</u> is the unconscious lowering of the bat at the beginning of the swing. This causes a variety of poor results, including an inordinate number of fly balls and pop-ups. Recommend drills that require the batter to keep his hands still at shoulder level at the beginning of the pitcher's delivery. The swing should be shortened and delayed with the objective of hitting a line drive or hard ground ball.

- <u>Uppercutting</u> results in fly balls and pop-ups by setting-up and swinging with the back shoulder too low. The hitter must be shown the advantages of holding the bat at shoulder height, with the shoulders level during the swing. The objective is to hit hard line drives rather than fly balls.

- <u>Topping</u> results in an inordinate number of ground balls that don't get through the infield. The hitter is swinging downward and/or hitting the top of the ball. Recommend re-emphasizing the need to track the ball from the pitcher's release point all the way to the hit zone. Also, stance and swing fundamentals should be reviewed.

- <u>Timing-</u> A late or early swing is a timing problem. Once again, the hitter not seeing the ball and its flight until well after the pitcher has released the ball can cause these problems. One-on-one offline drills with plastic golf balls and soft baseballs are recommended.

- A <u>lack of power</u> is caused by a variety of factors:
    - Insufficient strength
    - Lack of confidence
    - Arms not fully extended
    - Lack of aggressiveness
    - Psychological attitude

The recommended solutions include repetitious review of fundamentals and extra practice. Achievements should be publicly acclaimed. Problems should be addressed as privately as possible.

CHAPTER 7

PRACTICE - PRACTICE - PRACTICE ! ! !

As mentioned earlier, the most important fundamentals that should be taught are seeing the ball as it leaves the pitcher's hand (release point) and tracking the ball to the point of contact (hit zone). The difficulty is not in understanding but in execution. These fundamentals require more concentration than any other and consequently, if not executed properly, result in erratic hitting performance. One technique that helps is tossing ping-pong balls to the on-deck hitter to develop concentration and eye-to-hand coordination. Another technique is to have the pitcher roll a ball slowly toward the plate and then pitch another ball so that both balls arrive in front of the plate at approximately the same time. The "roll and pitch" technique forces the batter to ignore the rolled ball and concentrate intently on the pitched ball.

The objective is to convince the hitter that if he doesn't concentrate on tracking the ball throughout its entire trajectory, he will not hit the ball well. Once he is convinced, then he can start working on other fundamentals such as footwork, the swing, and making contact with the ball in the hit zone.

T-Ballers can practice concentration as well. The hitting coach can mark a number of practice balls with a black dot and set the ball on the Tee with the dot where the hitter should make contact. The hitter is successful if he hits a line drive into the back-stop or screen. This batting Tee drill can be used at any level, not only to improve concentration but also to practice stance set-up and swing elements. Some professional ball players use the batting Tee drill to discover and correct swing flaws throughout their careers.

CHAPTER 8

ORGANIZING PRACTICE SESSIONS

What is the best way to organize practices to maximize the use of available time and practice fields? There are too many variables to say that one way is better than all others. However, you might try the following and modify it to suit your situation. The most important thing is to keep every player busy every minute learning or practicing something. Figure 17 addresses the allotment of time within a two-hour practice session. It shows an example of how to maximize the time of four coaches and 12 players to get the most out of a two-hour practice period.

PRINCIPLES:
- Assign one coach to be the hitting coach and attempt to have him, and only him, give instruction.
- Have the hitting coach also instruct base running and other offensive subjects.
- Have the hitting coach run the offense (batting instruction, scoring strategy, signals, etc.)
- Teach fundamentals early preseason to the entire team in a classroom or indoor controlled environment.
- Reinforce training with demonstrations, illustrations and simple take-home handouts.

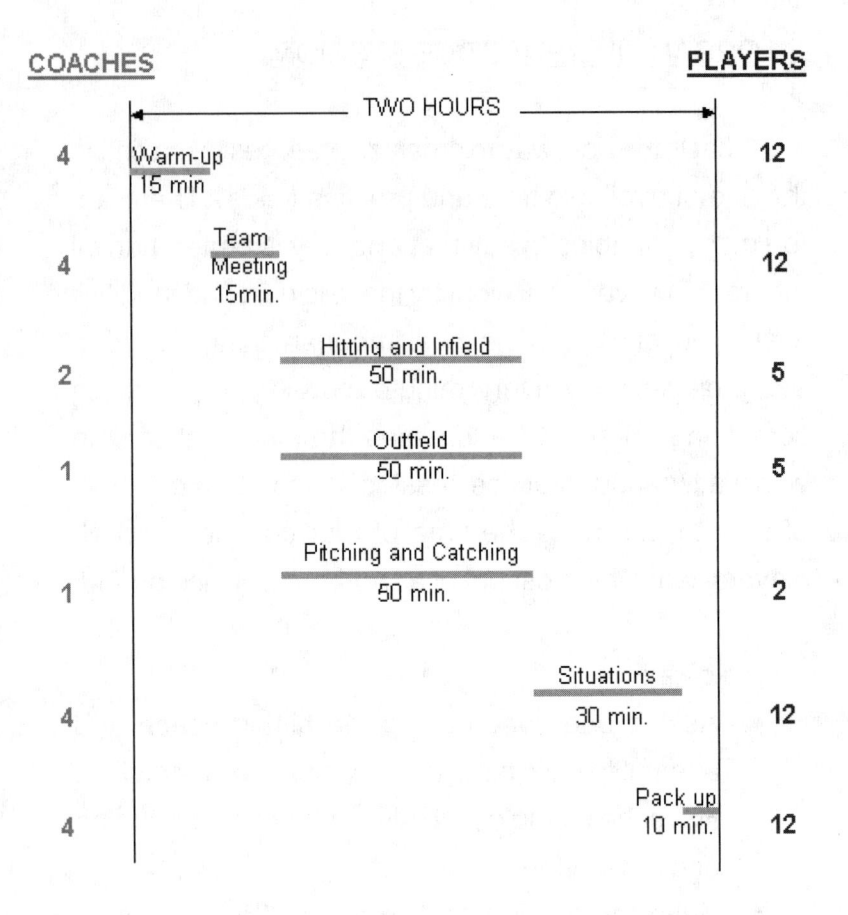

COACHES		PLAYERS
	←——— TWO HOURS ———→	
4	Warm-up 15 min	12
4	Team Meeting 15min.	12
2	Hitting and Infield 50 min.	5
1	Outfield 50 min.	5
1	Pitching and Catching 50 min.	2
4	Situations 30 min.	12
4	Pack up 10 min.	12

FIGURE 17

Practice Session Time Allotment

Develop a vocabulary when teaching fundamentals. Make sure all players understand meanings and don't vary them during the season.

EARLY PRESEASON FIELD PRACTICES:

- Break the team in half (approximately six players each half). One half for hitting, the other for fielding, pitching and catching (Figure 18).
- Use the backstop and infield for hitters and outfield and fringe areas for fielding, pitching and catching.
- Early preseason batting practice should be done without a catcher with the hitter against the backstop.
- Begin each hitting practice with a review of the fundamentals appropriate for the practice time available.
- Try to get a parent or volunteer to pitch hitting practice.
- The hitting coach should be near the hitter (left rear of right handed hitter) and talk to hitter as required (Figure 19).
- Remaining players in the group should take up defensive infield positions. The remaining players can either help the pitcher or be "on deck" to hit next.
- At mid-point in the practice session, exchange groups of players with the fielding coach and repeat hitting instruction.

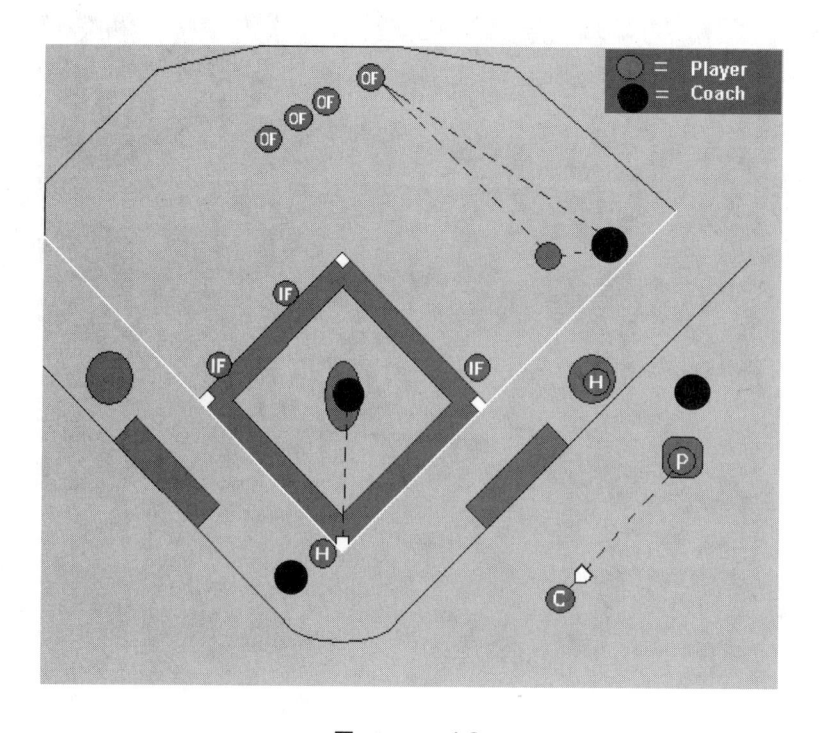

FIGURE 18

Practice Field Usage

FIGURE 19

Hitting Coach's Practice Position

LATER PRESEASON FIELD PRACTICES:
- Continue hitting instruction as in early preseason practices. Have an assistant coach spend extra time with players who are having trouble.
- Add a catcher to the hitting practice.
- Add base running to the hitting session.
- With the fielding coach and defensive players, practice game situations with three or four hitters/runners.

DURING IN-SEASON PRACTICES:
- Same as later preseason practice sessions except mix in team member pitchers with adults and volunteers.
- Continue to give extra help to hitters who are not doing well.
- Review those fundamentals that need reinforcement at every practice and before every game.

PRE-GAME WARM-UP:
- Within the thirty minutes normally available before the game, space and conditions permitting, get all players to participate in a slow jog/trot, some stretching and light calisthenics.
- Have hitters analyze the opponents' pitcher during their warm-up, with the intention of locating his release point.
- Have small groups (3 or 4 players) conduct bunting drills to enhance hand to eye coordination.

CHAPTER 9

SUMMARY:

- Coaches should explain the fundamentals of hitting so that all players understand what they are and how they should be properly applied in practices and in games. Players should be encouraged and commended when they learn and properly execute fundamentals.
- During initial training and practices, coaches should identify each player's hitting strengths and weaknesses. More time should be allotted to those who are having the most difficulty.
- Prior to every practice session, coaches should have a detailed plan to maximize the use of practice time. Practice fields and facilities are in great demand. Because of these limitations, the efficient use of practice facilities is essential. The sharing of practice fields with other teams and conducting scrimmage games is also recommended.
- In order to accomplish as much as possible during practice sessions, additional coaches are recommended. Try to get two or three additional practice coaches from parents and other volunteers. A minimum of four coaches should attend every practice in order to accomplish a

dynamic and fulfilling practice. 0
- Finally, the coaches and players objectives are to:
    - Have fun
    - Learn the individual skills required
    - Appreciate the value of teamwork
    - Develop friendships
    - Want to return to the program next season

The following points (Fig. 20) are a summary of the fundamental hitter's Stance Set-up and Swing Sequence elements. They are offered as a handy guide for coaches and players to attach to clipboards or copy for convenient distribution.

STANCE SET UP
POSITION IN BATTER'S BOX
GRIP
HANDS BACK AT SHOULDER LEVEL
KNEES SLIGHTLY BENT
HIPS AND SHOULDERS COILED
EYES FOCUSED ON RELEASE POINT
MAJORITY OF WEIGHT ON BACK FOOT
WRISTS COCKED

SWING SEQUENCE
SEE BALL LEAVE PITCHER'S HAND
TRACK BALL IN FLIGHT
START SWING
PUSH OFF BACK FOOT
UNCOIL HIPS AND SHOULDERS
STRIDE FORWARD WITH FRONT FOOT
REACH FOR BALL (IF IN HIT ZONE)
EXTEND ARMS FULLY
UNCOCK WRISTS AT CONTACT
FOLLOW THROUGH AFTER CONTACT

FIGURE 20

Summary of Stance and Swing Elements

COACH'S NOTES

COACH'S NOTES